Preparing for the CompTIA A+ certification can be a rewarding journey that equips you with foundational IT skills and knowledge. The A+ certification is highly regarded in the tech industry and can open doors to various job opportunities. To ensure success, a comprehensive study plan and effective strategies are essential. This guide will outline key steps and tips to help you prepare for the CompTIA A+ certification exam.

Understanding the CompTIA A+ Certification:

The CompTIA A+ certification is designed to validate your skills in IT operational roles and technical support. It covers a wide range of topics, including hardware, software, networking, mobile devices, cloud computing, and more. The certification is divided into two exams: Core 1 (220-1001) and Core 2 (220-1002). Each exam consists of multiple-choice questions, performance-based questions, and drag-and-drop questions.

Creating a Study Plan:

1. **Assessment:**

 Begin by assessing your current knowledge and skills. This will help you identify areas that require more attention and focus.

2. **Set Goals:**

 Set clear goals for your study plan. Determine when you want to take the exams and how much time you can dedicate to studying each day or week.

3. **Study Resources:**

 Gather study materials, such as textbooks, online courses, practice exams, and study guides. CompTIA offers official study resources on their website, including exam objectives and sample questions.

4. **Break It Down:**

 Divide the exam objectives into smaller topics and create a study schedule. Allocate more time to challenging areas and less time to topics you're already familiar with.

Effective Study Strategies:

1. **Hands-On Experience:**

 Practical experience is invaluable. Set up a lab environment with hardware and software components to practice troubleshooting and configuration tasks.

2. **Practice Exams:**

 Take practice exams to familiarize yourself with the format and types of questions. This will help you manage your time during the actual exam and identify weak areas.

3. **Flashcards:**

 Create flashcards to memorize technical terms, acronyms, and concepts. Regular review of flashcards can reinforce your memory.

4. **Study Groups:**

 Join or form study groups with fellow A+ candidates. Discussing topics, sharing insights, and solving problems together can enhance your understanding.

5. **Video Tutorials:**

 Watch video tutorials from reputable sources to grasp complex concepts visually. Visual aids can make understanding easier.

6. **Simulations:**

 Use interactive simulations to practice hands-on tasks. These simulations simulate real-world scenarios and allow you to apply your knowledge.

Time Management:

1. **Consistency:**
 Consistency is key. Dedicate a specific time each day or week for studying. Avoid cramming, as it's less effective than spaced-out learning.
2. **Time Blocks:**
 Divide your study time into manageable blocks, focusing on one topic at a time. This prevents burnout and promotes better retention.
3. **Review:**
 Regularly review previously studied material to reinforce your understanding and memory.

Test-Taking Strategies:

1. **Read Carefully:**

 During the exam, read each question and answer choice carefully. Pay attention to keywords that indicate what's being asked.

2. **Elimination:**

 Use the process of elimination to narrow down answer choices. Cross out obviously incorrect options to improve your chances of selecting the right one.

3. **Flagging:**

 If unsure about an answer, flag the question and move on. Answer questions you're confident about first, then return to flagged ones.

4. **Time Management:**

 Keep an eye on the time remaining for each section. Don't spend too much time on a single question.

<u>Staying Healthy and Relaxed:</u>

1. **Rest and Sleep:**

 Ensure you get adequate rest and sleep. A well-rested mind performs better during studying and exams.

2. **Healthy Lifestyle:**

 Eat nutritious meals, stay hydrated, and engage in regular physical activity. A healthy body supports cognitive function.

3. **Stress Management:**

 Practice stress-relief techniques such as deep breathing, or mindfulness. High stress levels can hinder your ability to learn and recall information.

 Preparing for the CompTIA A+ certification requires dedication, time, and a structured approach. By creating a comprehensive study plan, utilizing effective study strategies, and practicing good test-taking habits, you can increase your chances of success.

Remember that the A+ certification is not only about passing the exam but also gaining practical skills that will serve you well in your IT career. Stay focused, stay positive, and embrace the learning process.

We will include space below for your notes:

____

____

____

____

____

____